LEX SCHOLASTICUS JOURNAL OF LAW AND SOCIO-ECONOMIC ISSUES

VOLUME I, ISSUE I

LEX SCHOLASTICUS

ISBN 979-888530269-2

Contents

Editorial Note

Scholarly writing is an important part of the academic journey of any Law Student as it prepares the students for the journey ahead. Lex Scholasticus Journal of Law and Socio-Economic Issues has been started with an intent to make this experience a smooth one for our student friends. The journal has been established to promote the spirit of academic research, structured thinking and to provide the students with the courage to put their thoughts to the scrutiny by their peers.

It is important for legal scholars to have an opinion; it is equally important that the said opinion is always backed by facts and cogent logic. Scholarly writing helps foster these habits amongst students. The name Lex Scholasticus Journal of Law and Socio-Economic Issues also has been chosen to reflect this thought as it literally means student or scholar of Law. It is the endeavour of the editorial board of this journal to steer the contributing writers in the right direction by choosing thought provoking, timely and relevant topics to research and write upon. It is the objective of the editorial board to inculcate and nourish critical thinking amongst the contributing authors and the readers alike.

Sound research, cogent reasoning and astute writing are essential weapons in the arsenal of any law professional, and we earnestly believe that Lex Scholasticus Journal of Law and Socio-Economic Issues would help the student community in sharpening their skills. We hope to initiate and sustain meaningful dialogues through this journal and expect to be a valuable addition to the vast array of the renowned and reputed journals. On behalf of the Lex Scholasticus family, I invite our young scholars to be a part of this initiative and grow together with us as we start our journey in scholarly publishing.

"*__Adv. Akash Sinha__*
__(Editor in Chief)__"

CHAPTER ONE

Artificial Intelligence: A new trend for Traditional and Human laws - Parth Raman

From the Desk of the Editorial Board

Abstract:

Artificial intelligence could spell the end of the human race, says Hawking, yet, even utilized innovation for correspondence. Innovations ought to be in charge of humankind for a healthy lifestyle. This managing AI and law appears unexpectedly as the inspiration for a feasible future without upsetting the climate. It is inescapable that homo-sapiens are customized to get intrigued by the time of his developments.

Artificial intelligence is a science and a bunch of computational innovations that are motivated by the ways individuals utilize their sensory systems to detect, learn, reason, and make a move. Different areas are profited by these new advances yet on the opposite side worry is, these new innovations might be abused or put to unexpected and possibly hurtful ways. Today's issue on the part of the law in overseeing AI frameworks is more significant. How the law will battle to keep up the manners by which courts, policymakers and organizations are stepping in to stand up to the exceptional lawful and strategy questions introduced by the broad reception of AI. In this paper the specialist attempts to introduce top to bottom examinations of the lawful difficulties postured for AI frameworks.

Introduction:

Advances are developed to make routine life simple and smooth. The universe of innovation is changing quickly with PCs, machines and robots, supplanting basic human exercises. Artificial Intelligence(AI) is one such development. Generally, AI is a machine that can really think all alone. Simulated intelligence can be perceived as the ability of a machine to duplicate keen conduct. From a more extensive perspective, AI alludes to organically propelled data frameworks and incorporates complex advances like AI, profound learning, PC vision, regular language preparation, machine thinking and solid AI. Anyway AI identifies with the comparative assignment of utilizing PCs to comprehend human knowledge, however it doesn't restrict itself to techniques that are organically recognizable. All in all comprehension "Artificial Intelligence, a part of software engineering, is the entertainment of human knowledge measures by machines extraordinarily PC framework, means to make canny machines which can frequently act and respond like people and makes workable for PCs to perform undertakings including human-like dynamic, insight, learned abilities or aptitude.

Understanding of Artificial Intelligence:

An intelligent entity has five attributes i.e.,"(1) Communication, (2) Internal knowledge, (3) External knowledge, (4) Goal-driven behaviour and (5) Creativity." AI technology includes Machine Learning (ML), Cognitive Computing, Deep Learning, Predictive application programming interfaces (APIs), Natural Language Processing (NLP), Image Recognition, Speech Recognition etc. Highly technical, specialised skill and expert system is required in the process of Particular applications of artificial intelligence. AI includes programming of computers for certain characteristics such as: Knowledge, Reasoning, problem solving, Perception, Learning, Planning, and Ability to move objects. Knowledge Engineering and Machine learning are core parts of AI research. For a machine to act and react like a human, a machine must be possessed with accurate information about the world. To implement knowledge engineering AI is essentially to access properties, categories, objects and their relations. It is a tedious task to insert reasoning, power to solve problems and common sense in a machine. Machine learning and learning requires ample supervision with numerical regressions and classification. Machine perception is capable of using sensory inputs to interpret the different aspects of the world, while computer vision is the power to analyze visual inputs with a few sub-problems such as facial, object and gesture recognition.

Artificial intelligence innovation incorporates Machine Learning (ML), Cognitive Computing, Deep Learning, Predictive application programming interfaces (APIs), Natural Language Processing (NLP), Image Recognition, Speech Recognition and so forth Profoundly specialized, a specific aptitude and master framework is needed during the time spent particular uses of man-made brainpower. Artificial intelligence incorporates programming of PCs for specific attributes, for example, Knowledge, Reasoning, critical thinking, Perception, Learning, Planning, and Ability to move objects. Information Engineering and Machine learning are the centre portion of AI research. For a machine to act and respond like a human, it is an essential machine that must have precise data of the world. To actualize information designing AI is basically to get to properties, classes, items and their relations. It is a monotonous assignment to embed thinking, capacity to take care of issues and sound judgment in a machine. AI and learning requires adequate oversight with mathematical relapses and characterization. Machine observation is competent to utilize tactile contributions to decipher the various parts of the world, while PC vision is the ability to examine visual contributions with a couple of sub-issues, for example, facial, article and signal acknowledgment.

Law And AI:

Initially, Rules and guidelines that are to be trailed by individuals and if it's abused, the outcomes will be as discipline. Besides, man-made reasoning or machine insight is that machines are taken care of with data needed to respond, convey and to manage the circumstances.

Model (humanoids) for example robots as humans. Computer based intelligence with law becomes possibly the most important factor in different structures including law bots, legal decisions given by humanoids thus numerous different things for the decrease in manpower and precision of the work. Law taught with AI isn't that effectively versatile and satisfactory in this flexible and differentiated social country, despite the fact that westernization and modernization are assuming a noticeable part in this day and age. Still neediness in India has not been completely annihilated.

This advancement cycle can be acknowledged by elites and the high class individuals of the general public and not the lower or the center ones, albeit center ones are consistently in a confused mentality and can't get into both of the areas. The historical backdrop of law advancing from compositions to the present get-together of data about case status on the web, there has been a gigantic cycle and the time taken for it to hit the general public. Since AI requires high support and permit for it to be utilized, it takes an incredible range of abilities from man to look after it. A demonstration or legitimate system must be accomplished for the entire set up to occur.

The utilization of AI assumes a prevalent function in prescient coding where AI utilizes the calculations to gain from the named preparing instances of expectations and investigation of result. Hence AI and law can be utilized in light of the fact that to devour time, cash and it goes about as a decent substitute for misuse of paper. Law and AI becomes an integral factor in different field of law including law (for keeping everything protected in an information base) and it is likewise fluctuated contrasted and licensed innovation rights and further AI and law additionally helps in correcting quickly as per the changing cultural requirements since it can store , break down and give yield at whatever point vital.

This cycle isn't as dreary as the present where we store things and it requires some investment to look at or recognize. It accepts everything as manual where we can utilize AI and lessen the work pressure from it. Since India is additionally a nation which sets aside a long effort to discard the cases, AI would massively assist with lessening the time which gives both the gatherings and the adjudicator the alleviation right away.

BOT:

A Bot (short for robot) that works as a specialist and invigorates a human action. A Bot is a computerized application used to perform straightforward and redundant assignments that would be tedious, commonplace or outlandish for a human to perform. There are a number of reasons why law offices would need to utilize .Bots don't need any compensation, reward, an office or different costs that are needed for every lawyer.

I embrace a definition of a robot as a machine with three qualities they are as follows:

Robot can sense its environment.

Robot has the capacity to process the information.

Robot is organized to act directly upon its environment.

Law Bots:

Law bots are web indexes like talk bots that are generally utilized to explain questions of laymen without expenditure of financial assets. Law bots likewise helps in a manner for apprentices to gain from it. The law bots have unquestionably evolved in the US under (Bots act 2016) by Barack Obama.

It gives lawful thinking and furthermore clarifies the need and necessity of every person. There are additionally rising in India for which causes have been begun and it before long requires legal counselors likewise to work it. This decreases human work pressure and furthermore the serious issues of overlooking things become clear.

Changing Legal field:

As per advisors contemplating this issue, the ascent of AI would change the lawful field. Law offices would have the option to set aside cash changing to AI bots yet it is likewise conceivable that in the end customers will likewise not pay more than what AI work cost the firm. Bigger law offices would be bound to utilize AI bots and comparable innovation; more modest firms are additionally going to confront difficulties from administrations that give authoritative documents online to virtual law offices.

While, AI bots may appear to be even more sci-fi than reality today. The equivalent could be said for different devices, for example, prescient coding utilized vigorously in law offices. Because of different variables including the strain to cut charges and innovation the legitimate business is changing and firms need to basically adjust so as to remain serious.

Can Judicial Verdict Be Given By AI?

Legal decision or judgment given ought to be inside proportion decidendi, obiter announcement and gaze decisis as indicated by considerable law. Going to the need of AI in giving judgment is that standard of normal equity, which comprises two essential columns as per regulatory law.

Nemo in propria causa judex, esse debet (nobody should be made appointed authority in his own argument or the standard against inclination) Audi alteram partem (decide that nobody ought to be censured unheard)

Along these lines, as per first principle, there comes inclination of different sorts that include:

Monetary inclination;

Individual predisposition;

Topic predisposition;

Departmental predisposition;

Biased predisposition;

Predisposition dependent on persistence.

Despite the fact that these issues can be settled by Doctrine of need (rejects predisposition and bias).

There are a few cases that have been referred to for inclination of different kinds. We surmise if AI is working with making decisions without predisposition and bias and consequently equity could be delivered all the more without any problem. With help from some individual in power, an official choice can be given by AI, so the evident and reasonable nature of the choice could be reflected. There can't likewise be 100% flawlessness yet all in all this can lessen the responsibility of carelessness or error.

The well known and famous ROSS insight (lawful web crawler) is picking up such a great amount of consideration in US, comparative way numerous different nations are adjusting so many like IBM WATSON question noting PC framework which likewise can comprehend regular language, practice group is right now managing Amazon and Google to teach AI into its organization, additionally the one that spearheaded in the legitimate exploration is CASE MINE which is all the rage. Subsequently, it is getting created in different nations like the USA, Canada and others. In spite of the fact that there are a few thoughts continuing for improvement of AI, another gathering which exists is absolutely against utilization of a keen right hand.

Civil (Contract and Tort) Liability:

The more self-ruling AI applications are, the more troublesome it might be to hold singular creators or designers subject to the (undeniably less predictable) outcomes of AI exercises. This makes the normal guidelines on risk deficient and calls for new standards which center around how to decide if an AI application is liable for its demonstrations or oversight; and assuming this is the case, regardless of whether strategy contemplations in any case propose that the seller or the creator should bear the subsequent expense. In the event that the intention is to boost due consideration, a severe risk system supported by protection might be generally effective.

Past these prompt worries, as self-governing AI applications create, the principal question of whether AI ought to have a legitimate status might be tended to by administrators around the world. The issue of AI self-rule would bring up the issue of its temperament in the light of the current lawful classifications – of whether it should be viewed as common individual, legitimate individual, creature or item – or whether another class ought to be made, with its own particular highlights and suggestions as respects the attribution of rights and obligations, including risk for harm. In contrast to enactment, the security gave by the courts is healing not deterrent. Courts survey risk and harms dependent on earlier lawful point of reference. Situations where the damage is asserted to have been brought about by AI applications request that the court unwind novel innovation and apply sick fitting case law to make judgments of obligation. For instance, US precedent-based law misdeed and misbehavior guarantees regularly focus on human focused ideas of deficiency, carelessness, information, goal, and sensibility. What happens when human thinking is supplanted by an AI application. What happens when the culprit or the casualty is AI?

IP Laws and Artificial Intelligence:

The innovativeness and information shown by AI frameworks is unmistakably obvious to the world and concerns with respect to IP insurance has unquestionably grown in the brains of individuals upholding rights according to licensed innovation. Consequently, we should investigate more deliberative finishes of copyright and patent laws regarding AI frameworks.

These days there are machines that make exceptionally imaginative works that would be qualified for copyright security in the event that they were made by people. This requires a reconsideration of copyright guidelines for AI frameworks everywhere in the world. As of late a San Francisco Court in Naruto v Slater held that, creatures by excellence of the way that they are not people need locus standi under Copyright Act to sue for encroachment.

The Bench of Carlos T. Bea and N. Randy Smith, Circuit Judges, and Eduardo C. Robreno, District Judge, while settling on the issue whether a monkey can sue for harms and injunctive alleviation for copyright encroachment, held that, the monkey specifically and all creatures all in all, by ideals of the way that they are not people, do not have the legal locus standi under the Copyright Act, despite the fact that they have a protected remaining under Art. III of the United States Constitution. The Court thought that, since the Copyright Act doesn't explicitly approve creatures to record copyright encroachment suits, Naruto, the monkey can't sue for copyright encroachment.

With copyright for creatures good and gone, a comparable circumstance has emerged for AI frameworks. As of now, machine created works are not enlisted by numerous individuals of the copyright workplaces over the world. A comparable issue has emerged on account of patent laws. On the off chance that the curiosity measures under patent law is satisfied by machines, issues identifying with responsibility for innovations will emerge. Additionally, can responsibility for developments be given to the robots/machines? In the event that AI counterfeits a creation or repeats a development, by what method can encroachment and harms be resolved? These are a portion of the easily proven wrong issues that emerge as for AI and IP laws.

Indian IP Laws:

Enactments like the Copyright Act, 1957 and Patents Act, 1970 will have suggestions to AI frameworks in India. In this paper certain parts of the previously mentioned acts are figured out and its effect on AI is examined.

Certain arrangements in these demonstrations frequently go about as barricades in the advancement of these AI frameworks and denies IP assurance to the works delivered by these machines. Ample opportunity has already passed that these institutions are corrected to oblige further developed and refined advancements.

Copyright Act, 1957 and AI:

The sine qua non of copyright is inventiveness. Innovation is a precondition to copyright insurance. A work is conceded just when it is unique for example it isn't replicated from some other work. It isn't even important that the work ought to include novel articulation of an idea. Everything necessary for creativity of articulation is that the articulation ought not be replicated from another work. Subsequently the work ought to be formed by the creator freely.

There are two tenets identified with the trial of creativity of a work. They are:

I) Sweat of the Brow Doctrine.

ii) Modicum of Creativity.

As indicated by the Sweat of the Brow Doctrine, a creator can get a copyright on his work by utilizing straightforward industriousness. There is no prerequisite of considerable inventiveness or innovation. He is qualified for a copyright just by virtue of endeavors and cost put in by him in the making of such a work.

As per Modicum of Creativity, inventiveness stays alive in a work where an adequate measure of scholarly innovativeness and judgment has gone into the formation of that work. The level of inventiveness need not really be high however a base degree of imagination ought to be guaranteed for copyright security.

The Indian Courts have received the pinch of imagination test on account of Eastern Book Company v D.B. Modak. After an exhaustive perusal of this convention underscored in the previously mentioned judgment, it can't be said that AI frameworks can't accomplish a speck of innovativeness. Accordingly, crafted by these machines can finish the assessment of inventiveness.

An arrangement under the Copyright Act, 1957 which represents a test to copyright assurance to works of AI frameworks is Section 2 (d) of the demonstration. This part characterizes the term 'creator'. For responsibility for copyrighted work, the individual should fall under the ambit of an "creator". This is perplexing for AI since they are by and large not viewed as a lawful individual.

As indicated by Section 2 (d) "creator" signifies,-

(vi) corresponding to any scholarly, sensational, melodic or aesthetic work which is PC created, the individual who makes the work be created;"

The issue under this definition is the expression 'the individual who makes the work be made'. For an individual to make a work be made near the individual with the work is significant and with the end goal of this demonstration individual here methods a human or a lawful individual. Subsequently, the current Copyright Act isn't comprehensive of AI frameworks. In this manner, with regards to works that are made by AI, their creation would be conflicted under Indian Copyright Laws.

Licenses Act, 1970 And AI:

Segment 2 (p) of the Patents Act, 1970 characterizes the expression "patentee".

"Patentee" means a person for the time being entered on the register as the grantee of proprietor of the patent.

Section 2 (t) characterizes "individual intrigued".

"Individual intrigued" incorporates an individual occupied with, or in advancing, research in a similar field as that to which the innovation relates.

Section 6 recommends the rundown of people who can apply for a patent.

(a) Any individual professing to be the valid and first creator of the invention.

Section 2 (y) of the demonstration characterizes the expression "valid and first designer".

It does exclude either the initial shipper of a development into India, or an individual to whom a creation is first imparted from outside India.

Segment 2 (y) doesn't explicitly express that the "valid and first designer" should be a human and along these lines it can be viewed as giving an extension to the incorporation of works by AI frameworks.

However, since the definitions for terms like "patentee", "individual intrigued" and so forth express that it should be an individual (a lawful individual), the aim of the lawmaking body for the universally useful demonstration can be perceived to be preferring people and other legitimate people. Subsequently, it is significant that these institutions should be corrected so as to suit the necessities of the advancing society and logical frameworks.

India is an agricultural nation and it will in any case stay a non-industrial nation if such important corrections are not made to establishments in an exceptionally powerful field like protected innovation. These are not fantastical objectives for a nation like India.

The Need for a Policy system for Governing AI:

As there are no arrangement rules for managing AI in India, it might in the long run pull in lawful and moral issues concerning its application. In this way, the need to have an approach structure for organizations (while demonstrating and coding AI) and the administration to meet the lawful and moral guidelines, can be tended to by principally settling on the idea of element an AI framework is, and appropriately the obligation could possibly be moved from its makers to the AI framework which practices some level of restraint. This might be examined by drawing a relationship among AI and enterprises, in order to comprehend the similitude, assuming any, between how AI, on one hand, and an organization, as a counterfeit individual, then again, functions. In the sci-fi, I, Robot, Asimov (1950, p. 40) set down three broadly examined entrancing laws for robots,which are clashing in nature, managing, by and large, restrictions on robots making hurt people in various circumstances.

The dread against present day trend setting innovation is somewhat on the grounds that AI applications are not dependent upon any law under most purviews. I, Robot and other artistic works have indicated how in future AI may present extreme dangers to mankind, if unregulated. Comparable feelings of trepidation were held when partnerships appeared concerning the wide range of offenses it might submit. In the long run, various standards, for example, change conscience teaching, coordinating brain hypothesis, lifting of the corporate cloak, and so on, came to be applied to decide corporate risk. Consequently, planning standards which focus the risk of AI substances in circumstances which are plausible and predictable outcomes of the use of such innovation in different fields, starting today and, sooner rather than later, is exceptionally basic. The AI apparatus ought to be so planned as to empower it to figure out what is reasonable; yet in addition recognize, assess and right inclination inside the boundaries set somewhere near its human-client. This will bring about norms of an ideal, just and reasonable society.

Part of attribution of lawful personhood to AI element in the assurance of its risk:

The subject of finding out risk, both common and criminal, of an AI element, parallelly encroaches upon whether legitimate personhood might possibly be allowed upon it. Kurki and Pietrzykowski (2017) banter over the idea of lawful personhood against the foundation of its good and lawful applications on the scenery of regulating statute. They talk about how monetary and down to earth reasons might be the reason for giving lawful personhood upon programming operators. The ideas of 'personism' and 'personalism' are analyzed, and it is called attention to how character might be isolated from mankind. The association between lawful personhood, mankind and legitimate character is investigated.

The attribution of lawful personhood has been tended to by Kelsen (1945) in his hypothesis of character, as indicated by which, giving of legitimate personhood is just a 'specialized representation' to state rights, obligations and liabilities. The hypothesis infers that lawful personhood of an element is, when all is said in done, a legitimate gadget to sort out its privileges and liabilities. In light of the Hohfeldian examination of rights, each privilege has a comparing obligation as its journal correlative. In the light of a jurisprudential investigation of these speculations, whether or not robot rights and liabilities might be appropriately stated by allowing them legitimate personhood is analyzed. Allowing lawful personhood may, thus, bring about restricted obligation for the people worried about assembling or programming or working the AI framework. It is contended that, maybe, now of time when the innovation is as yet being created and tested in fresher fields, allowing lawful personhood to an AI element for learning risk may not be vital so as to make it subject.

Suggestions:

Since everything is getting automated, it would be valued if graduate schools incorporate AI alongside computers as a subject with the goal that youths can find out about legitimate coding techniques and utilization of AI for everyday practice purposes.

For a decent beginning and for picking up individuals' acknowledgment and more like experimentation strategy, we can utilize AI for street rules. As we probably are aware thruways mishaps continue expanding step by step and it very well may be controlled or held under check by sensors utilizing AI for checking as far as possible and prompt move can be made.

This could be the most significant one, discard electronic waste in a more proficient way since they produce more destructive synthetic compounds than other plastic squanders. This must likewise happen in a procedural way and in its cycle it must not influence the climate.

In our nation they can make enactment or any guideline about the utilization of AI (as given in the US by Barack Obama in the year 2016 BOTS ACT). This way it could assist all the residents with thinking about this.

All the entire, primary point is to diminish destitution and become a created country, so organizations can lead mindfulness programs about AI to poor or end of the week areas of the general public and it can likewise be remembered for CSR of the organization. The organizations can likewise make humanoids and they can likewise encourage the unskilled people like SOPHIA (humanoid robot).

Utilizing gifted representatives for the taking control and care of humanoids created can make business open doors for skilled ones.

In a characteristic manner, geothermal energy is the most ideal approach to deliver power which assumes the major significant part in the use of robots, and new ways can likewise be found normally for creation of power.

Mining is hazardous after certain profundity, where they can send self driving trucks and automated drills and along these lines the demise of individuals during mining can be dropped down.

Shows can be made at worldwide level and settlement can likewise be marked as given for space, air laws and so forth, this could make it more clear for all the nations to have a ceasefire.

In spite of the fact that this may digress from the point, India is an agro-based nation, so for manual work AI can be instilled and assignments can be made simpler for ranchers of our nation and in any event, for assurance of nation, rather than soldier there can be humanoids which could withstand extraordinary climate and can assault with all the more weighty weapons.

Effective IT Law:

In the event of a break of Data security system, who is to be accused without human intercession, on the grounds that the information assurance system in India is alarmingly powerless to coordinate the movement of development of AI. Comprehensively, the Information Technology Act, 2000 is the main bit of enactment which 'addresses' this subject. Though it is unquestionable that specific shields relating to information assurance and security have been set down in Sections 43 A and 72 of the Act, yet the protections miss the mark concerning guaranteeing genuine insurance as a result of the dark idea of arrangements, added significantly through alterations. It raises the requirement for thorough information insurance enactment in India, on the lines of European Directive on Data Protection, UK Data Protection Act (1998), OECD Guidelines on the Protection of Privacy and Transborder Flows of Personal Data, 1980, and the Safe Harbor standards of the US. Furthermore, the legislature must set up satisfactory protections as earlier hints of extraction of data to singular clients i.e., to the wellspring of data.

Parallel Approach:

Artificial intelligence is the future and there is no refusal, yet in our journey of replacing 'human mistakes' with savvy innovation and solid AI, we have to move moderately and stay informed concerning the equal necessities of overhauling the laws and scholarly structure in the nation.

Two-layered insurance model:

Since 2017, in excess of 20 nations (counting, India) have delivered conversation papers on AI. In any case, till date, no nation has ordered a particular enactment to exhaustively manage the utilization of AI. Accordingly, to be at the front line of this upset, the Indian council should find a way to fill the administrative lacunae and give guarantee in this field. Artificial intelligence is developing multi-crease innovation and we don't have the foggiest idea about all the preferences or threats related to it. In this manner it is of most extreme significance to have a two-layered insurance model: one-mechanical controllers; and two-laws to control AI activities just as for responsibility for blunders.

Conclusions:

As of now we rely upon some type of AI consistently. Siri, for instance, is a frail AI framework utilized by numerous individuals to assist them with night in everyday errands. It is a frail AI framework on the grounds that the yield from this framework is completely constrained by the developer. We additionally have solid AI frameworks like "Creativity Machine" utilized by the U.S military to plan weapons, these are frameworks which have inventive reasoning and high consistent thinking capacities.

Numerous unpredictable types of AI frameworks that make human life a lot simpler is around the bend and we can't stand to disregard these turns of events. Artificial intelligence frameworks will assume control over the world sooner rather than later. This change in outlook has gotten inescapable for mankind.

Sophia was created by Hanson Robotics, a Hong Kong based organization. Sophia turned into the primary robot to get citizenship of any nation. Sophia turned into a resident of Saudi Arabia. This denoted the start of a period of robot residents. The general public and the enactment overseeing it ought to be well prepared to oblige such progressive changes.

Soon, crafted AI frameworks can't be denied IP insurance exclusively based on the contention that they are not people or legitimate people. To deny them the rights enforceable by any resident of any nation will add up to an encroachment of their privileges.

Comprehensive development later on will mean the consideration of each type of logical progressions. This implies that even robots/machines/ AI frameworks should be important for this development. A world conveyed on AI is a predetermination picked by people and it will be desirable to be fittingly ready for this time of science where it isn't simple fiction. It is the ideal opportunity for another world renaissance.

Reference:

Roger C. Schank, "what is AI, anyway?", American Association for Artificial Intelligence Menlo Park, CA, USA, Volume 8 Issue 4, Winter 1987,Pages 58 - 65

Artificial Intelligence Litigation: Can the Law Keep Pace with The Rise of the Machines?, at http://www.quinnemanuel.com/the-firm/news-events/ article-december-2016-artificial-intelligence-litigation-can-the-law-keep-pace-with-the-rise-of-the-machines/.

Mukherjee, S. (2018, July 20). Applications of Artificial Intelligence (AI) In Business. [Blog post] Retrieved from https://www.hackerearth.com/ blog/developers/applications-of-artificial-intelligence/

Nilsson, N.J. (2009). The quest for artificial intelligence: A history of ideas and achievements. New York, NY: Cambridge University Press.

https://na.theiia.org/periodicals/Public%20Documents/GPI-Artificial-Intelligence-Part-III.pdf

Roger C. Schank, "what is AI, anyway?", American Association for Artificial

Intelligence Menlo Park, CA, USA, Volume 8 Issue 4, Winter 1987,Pages 58 - 65

https://www.tractica.com/newsroom/press-releases/artificial-intelligence

https://www.techopedia.com/definition/190/artificial-intelligence-ai

http://caribou.in/artificial-intelligence.php

http://www.legalserviceindia.com/legal/article-157-ways-in-which-artificial-intelligence-is-transforming-copyright-law.html

CRIME PREVENTION: WHAT CAN THE GOVERNMENT DO TO LOWER THE CRIME RATES - SHASHWAT SINGH

<u>Student of Chandigarh University, Mohali.</u>

It is critical to develop a technique that may successfully mediate the pattern of brutality before it claims the future in order to reduce wrongdoing and refresh networks. Along these lines, a key focus of our efforts should be to reach and advise our country's youth, who, by the age of 18, are confronted with more major good choices than their parent's generation faced in a lifetime. There is a model for persuading teenagers to intervene. There are many people around the country who have proved their capacity to provide assistance and serve as role models for in-danger teens. The relevance and innovative power of these dedicated local community pioneers may best be appreciated when understanding the scope of current youth challenges and the tragic history of countless regular, carefully structured programs for at-risk adolescents. Violations committed by teenagers around the country, who commonly express an uncomfortable sensation of rage, have raised public awareness that a part of the population is in need of help. Reports and measured tests also reveal that the scourge of unearthly pain and harshness is anything but a contained "downtown" issue and that it affects people of all income levels. As internal city adolescents, young people from rural areas and regional networks are wasting, losing, and ending their lives across the country. Every year, 5,000 children die as a result of an attack, illness, or suicide. It is expected that one in every seven young people between the ages of ten and eighteen will escape their homes. Every year, 1.5 million children live on the streets.

As a source of income, many of these children turn to the drug trade or prostitution. Patterns in juvenile social decisions show that if credible mediation and support are not provided, the emergency will worsen. In a recent survey of eighth-graders, 33 percent claimed they use illicit drugs, and 15 percent claimed they had broken more than five alcoholic beverages in a row in the preceding two weeks. In 1996, the greatest increase in births to young persons was too young females under the age of 15. Between 1985 and 1992, the rate of gun murder among 10- to 14-year-olds more than tripled, while the rate of self-destruction within this age group increased by 120 percent. 5 Clearly, our country's traditional responses to issues of juvenile savagery have not been successful, despite the vast sums of money that have been invested in them. Analysts predict that teenager arrests for heinous crimes will increase by 2010. According to a new cross-country study, posse involvement in the United States has grown to more than 650,000 youths affiliated with 25,000 groups.

As a result, the FBI launched a massive crackdown, deploying 133 teams around the country, resulting in around 92,000 arrests and 35,000 convictions during a four-year period. However, in a number of cases, these arrests came dangerously close to relocating a "bubble" of crime to another location. According to one prison guard in a state where a sizable proportion of the 38,000-person prison population has been identified as gangsters, "The problem does not go away. When the neighborhood disposes of its pack issue, it is transferred to the restorative institution. Indeed, it appears to be more intense."

Until now, most resources and efforts to safeguard our country's children have been directed at urban People in the city center. Because their networks do not have the monetary reliability, children in low-income areas have faced the most severe impact of the good free-fall that is afflicting the cutting edge. In disciplines like as posse action, unwed adolescents Many of the most successful problem solvers are persons who have personally faced and overcome the challenges they push others to overcome, such as parenting and substance abuse. Their step by step lives give a sensible representation of the characteristics and standards they advance, and their reliable, long stretch commitment to the youths they serve has won the sureness, trust, and respect of young people, even the people who had been considered hopeless by the social assistance circumstance.

Ignoring their reasonability, all things considered, rules have steadily denied such grassroots volunteers from giving organizations in their neighborhoods since they need educational degrees or master affirmation. "Saving" a young person from their environment may not be the game plan. The rescue technique for customary ventures ignores the value-creating, interceding developments that exist inside the youngsters' own organizations (families, neighborhood affiliations, etc) and may, to be sure, attack and usurp them. It is relied upon to be that the game plan lies in the worth of the people who are outside the neighborhood. This is veritable even of the much-praised manage ideal for grams, which every so often evade watchmen and neighbors. What message does a youth traverse programs that are based on the arrangement that genuine models ought to be brought into their homes what's more, organizations?

The presence of young people can't be protected through an outside intervention that ignores the need of supporting and sustaining their organizations. The best approach to setting up reliable and functional assistance lies in using the local, "standard antibodies" of a neighborhood, can stay away from social infection. Zeroing in on a solitary area of a complex of interrelated issues may not work. Then again, singular region-based exertion tends to the whole individual and the interrelated variables that impact a person's life. For example, extraordinary compared to other substance abuse programs I have encountered, the San Antonio-based Victory Cooperation, doesn't focus just on destroying medicine and alcohol obsession yet also unites tasks to rejoin and sustain families, meet the necessities of the posterity of addicts, and give informational and work openings. Through Victory Fellowship's incredible Christian version of the Boy Scouts, the Royal Rangers, youths who have adequately crushed their addictions fill in as genuine models for young fellows age additionally, more prepared, overseeing them in endeavors of the neighborhood and local area obligation. Lately, a planned exertion of grassroots exercises in Washington called Hands Across DC has made a model expansive framework.

Five social affairs have joined to 'jump profound' into tormented areas, supporting the overcomers of homicide casualties, planning kept men to fulfill their obligations to their families and organizations, moreover, giving beneficial activities and informative openings for adolescents. Local, grassroots, youth mediation strong of grams all through the Nation have shown us that responses for this crisis exist. Neighborhood-based approaches have been strikingly incredible in dispensing with rather than simply dislodging youth violence. Records of their undertakings show us, regardless, that there is no substitute method to impelling the adjustment of adolescents' vision and characteristics. Such inside changes are the harvest of long stretch reliable effort, constant availability, and the individual delineation of adults who have submitted themselves to a calling to safeguard young lives. Crime prevention is a big issue that must be addressed. It is simpler to obtain a full knowledge of the topic by focusing on one sort of crime in a case study and the numerous attempts undertaken to prevent and reduce its existence in society. Domestic violence is defined in Section 3 of the Protection of Women from Domestic Violence Act of 2005 as verbal, sexual, emotional, physical, and economic abuse of a woman. It is worth noting that the Act defines phrases such as "aggrieved person," "woman," and "shared household," among others.

According to WHO research, more than one in every three women worldwide experience some form of domestic violence-physical or sexual, making this a public health concern of epidemic proportions. However, the research also indicates that this problem may be averted, as proven by a few pilot studies. Combining socio-economic variables such as improved education systems, decreased male alcohol usage, maintaining a consistent pay structure, and confronting the problem through a formal and robust judicial procedure may result in a lower incidence rate. Male dominance, for example, is a cultural impact. Gender power dynamics are another issue that must be addressed in order to reduce incidences of domestic violence. To combat this threat, a huge increase on all of the above-mentioned fronts is required. A life devoid of violence is a fundamental expectation and the rightful right of every individual—man, woman, or kid. Domestic abuse is an epidemic, and the COVID 19 pandemic is bringing new issues for humankind globe. With most nations implementing total lockdown to control the infection and reduce illness and mortality, women are bearing the brunt of the damage. The lockdown is locking up women who have abusive spouses and, more dangerously, isolating them from social and community services that they might normally seek as a method of escape.

Social isolation makes it difficult to reach out to victims in need of assistance. It has been noticed that pandemics, epidemics, wars, and conflicts of any kind disproportionately affect women and make them easy victims. While Chinese government authorities say that domestic violence cases increased in the month COVID-19 first emerged, the BBC reported that an estimated 1.6 million women and 786000 men suffered domestic abuse in England and Wales in the fiscal year ending March 2019. Since the outbreak of the pandemic, the number of women seeking refuge in women's shelters in Denmark has also grown. Similar incidents have been reported in Greece, Brazil, Germany, Italy, Cyprus, Spain, and Australia. Furthermore, reports indicate that lockdowns have made it nearly difficult for women to get emergency contraception. In the absence of the lockdown, the United Nations Population Fund (UNFPA) predicts that over 7 million unwanted births will occur. In light of the catastrophic situation, several of these nations have already called for reforms in-laws and regulations. A prosecutor in Italy also ordered that in cases of domestic violence, the culprit, not the victim, must leave the home—especially vital during this pandemic. Such a clause, however, already exists in the Indian Act. In Germany, legislative leader Katrin Göring-Eckardt asked authorities to explore converting vacant hotels and guest homes into safe havens for women who are vulnerable at home during these difficult times.

Reference:

1. https://edubirdie.com/blog/criminal-justice-research-topics
2. https://blog.ipleaders.in/crime-prevention-india/
3. https://www.oxfordhandbooks.com/
4. https://www.unodc.org/

PAKISTAN AND CHINA ARE IN THE FRONT ROW OF THE NUCLEAR ASSEMBLY, LEAVING BEHIND INDIA - MEHAK

Student of Chandigarh University, Mohali.

Overview:

Why today is China increasing its nuclear weapons today, when all the nations are dismantling it? The clear cut answer is 'intention'. The tension which has aroused on the Line of Actual Control, is pretty much visible to every citizen of all around the globe. Are we equipped enough with warheads?

All the nations including developed, developing and rooted one, are modernising with better nuclear technology not for the sake of the war but adding on in for positive growth also. As reported by the eminent Swedish Think Tank; that India and China are trying to increase their nuclear reserve and moreover China has successfully succeeded in this act.

Not only nuclear arsenal but missiles including new land, sea based and nuclear capable aircraft. India and Pakistan are not capable of increasing it promptly. According to the report China had gone up from 290 to 320 nuclear warheads in the year 2019 to 2020 respectively. But till 2020, India has got only 150 nuclear arsenal, which is pretty low as compared to Pakistan having an estimated 160 warheads in the year 2020.

Movements of the Nation:

Basically, there are nine nuclear states in the world. They are the U.S., Russia, the United Kingdom, France, China, India, Pakistan, Israel and North Korea. Observe the tragedy, that the dictator state of North Korea is having nuclear warheads but the democratic state which is the Republic of South Korea is not having a nuclear arsenal. More or less, in 2019 there are 13,400 and later on in 2020 there are 13,865. The fall in number is due to the dismantlement of nuclear warheads by the U.S. and Russia. They both together possess a total 90% of nuclear warheads.

Actually, there is no such reliable data available by any government which owns nuclear warheads; about their nuclear arsenal. We can see that in today's diplomatic society no state wants to reveal its power in any field including nuclear warheads. For example; India has a National Security Act, 1980 which talks about confidential data regarding security of state. In the same way Pakistan also has specific laws regarding this issue. In the past few years, we have seen that the U.S. has disclosed the important credentials but after 2019 with due regulation passed by the Congress of the U.S. they also put an end to this disclosure. But in the case of Democratic People's Republic of Korea, the honorable dictator used his nuclear power to showcase his supremacy. So he usually publicises its data on nuclear warheads.

In the year 2010, a landmark treaty was signed between the U.S. and Russia which has been named as New Strategic Arms Reduction Treaty which is a pact about agreement to dismantlement of nuclear warheads. But the agreement will be null and void after February 2021. However, in a situation if both will agree then the time tenure of this treaty can be easily extended. According to many political scientists; firstly, the U.S. wants to increase this treaty to avoid the supremacy of Russia in nuclear power. Secondly, the U.S. and many more nations also want China to join this treaty to reduce its nuclear arsenal. Thirdly, Israel can also dominate in the nuclear field, so they also have to be there in the treaty partially.

Separately. India is also working on the same agenda of the dismantlement of nuclear warheads and this is totally correct according to the various suggestions of the International Court of Justice and United

Nations Human Rights Council and the theories of the ideal states but what about diplomatic and military point of view?

Leaving the things apart there are some laws binding and non binding like Nonproliferation Treaty (Non Member State), The Comprehensive Nuclear-Test-Ban Treaty (Member State), Fissile Material Cut-off Treaty (Member State) which initiate the gearing up process of dismantlement of the nuclear warheads in Republic of India. Meanwhile, the Islamic State of Pakistan has no such treaties with them and the same goes to China as well. Following these treaties India has not such rapid growth in the production of nuclear warheads but the scenario is not the same in atomic energy. We have seen that India has dominated in Asia after China, in promoting the electricity generation with the help of nuclear power.

We have to establish this only, having a nuclear arsenal doesn't mean that you are a big brother. The idea of nuclear energy was regulated by the founding fathers of the nations for the right of defence and concentrating on the productive issues. That's why, the Bhabha Atomic Research Centre (BARC) located in Mumbai, India which was led by our former Prime Minister Pt. Jawahar Lal Nehru works magnificently on productive management.

Conclusion; with progressive idea

Firstly, there should be a multilateral agreement in which all the nuclear states as well as spectator states will be a part of. The mentioned treaty will clearly say that; there should be limited nuclear warheads, modification will not reform it more draconian and violation of the terms quoted by the treaty will lead to hefty penalties.

Secondly, the simultaneous multilateral treaty will work on the dismantlement of nuclear warheads referring to the U.S., Russia and China.

Thirdly, in the Indian perspective; we need to develop diplomatic nuclear blocs with the nuclear states such as Russia, Israel, the United Kingdom and France.

Fourthly, we have to come up with the most active and enriched nuclear energy plants to make a productive use of nuclear power. It should be in a planned and phased manner.

CHAPTER FOUR

HUMAN RIGHTS FOR TODAY - SHUBHI SHARMA

Alumni, ICFAI Law School '20

This summer, the UN declared that it considers the internet to be a human right. Specifically, an addition was made to Article 19 of the Universal Declaration of Human Rights (UDHR), which states: "Everyone has the right to freedom of opinion and expression; this right includes freedom to hold opinions without interference and to seek, receive and impart information and ideas through any media and regardless of frontiers." Section 32 adds "The promotion, protection and enjoyment of human rights on the Internet" and another 15 recommendations that cover the rights of those who work in and rely on internet access. It also applies to women, girls, and those heavily impacted by the digital divide.

There were several countries opposed to the amendments, including Russia, China, Saudi Arabia, Indonesia, India and South Africa. These countries contested language that condemned any measures to disrupt internet access or hinder the sharing of information online. However, this language was crucial to the document's implementation and was approved in spite of opposition.

What Does Article 19 Mean For Countries Imposing Internet Shutdowns?

Article 19 is still considered a "soft" law in that it only recommends actions for nation-states and lacks any enforcement mechanisms as a "hard" law would. Before Article 19 came into being, an initial UN report on the Promotion and Protection of the Right to Freedom of Opinion and Expression was released to stop France and the UK from blocking copyright infringers from using the internet. It also opposes the blocking of internet access in retaliation to political unrest. The release also coincided with a shutdown of Syria's internet connection. The report aimed to set new standards for countries looking to follow in the footsteps of Syria and other countries during times of unrest in the future.

These were not the only instances of internet shutdowns since the report's release. Since January 2015, there have been 35 recorded cases of internet shutdowns. One of the most recent shutdowns happened in October in southeast Turkey during protests against the detention of a Turkish mayor and co-mayor. Of the 35 countries imposing shutdowns, no governments have since renounced the practice, though Ghana recently promised not to shut down the internet during their 2016 election and Morocco has reversed the ban on video based applications in the country.

Though not enforceable, a UN resolution does hold some weight for countries actively working to curb corruption and gain more credibility with their citizens. Upholding the right to internet access is just one of many ways in which governments can begin rebuilding relationships with their citizens. There have been strides from countries and organizations alike to curtail the trend of increasing internet shutdowns. There is hope that the renouncing of internet shutdowns will grow and continue to gain traction on an international scale.

Pathway To The Future

A global and open internet is crucial to achieving the Agenda 2030 Sustainable Development Goals (SDGs), something recognized by Article 19 and demonstrated by the actions of organizations and countries alike. The SDGs aim to create partnerships among countries, and the protection and promotion of the internet could be a key way to unite stakeholders. Though the SDGs are non-binding, 193 UN members signed and adopted the document as part of a commitment to improving the 17 listed areas of which access to the internet stands to have a significant role in. Goals that focus on economic and social growth, such as Goals 8-11, and goals that focus on peace and partnerships, such as Goals 16-17, are a few where the internet can have a strong impact on implementation and service provision.

In a world where internet shutdowns are increasing year to year, it is important that the right steps are taken to improve the relationship between governments and citizens and to uphold all human rights. The UN could advance the cause of universal internet access by using the SDGs as a stepping stone; those whose livelihoods depend on internet access or who fear that their access will be terminated will have the most to gain. The 193 signatory countries have already committed to improving internet quality, sustainability, and accessibility—a first step to internet access truly being treated as a human right.

Currently, there are only 32 countries deemed to be resilient to Internet shutdowns. The other countries lack coverage options if a few providers shut down. For example, the Syrian government can easily shut down the country's single internet provider. Holding governments accountable for human rights violations, including restricting internet access, will advance reforms for protecting other human rights. More groups will advocate for the rights of individuals who lack reliable internet access, and more groups will organize to stop internet shutdowns.

References:

1. Article 10 protects your right to hold your own opinions (Equality and Human Rights Commission; Accessed on 06 Dec, 2021) https://www.equalityhumanrights.com/en/human-rights-act/ article-10-freedom-expression
2. The Internet as a Human Right (Catherine Howell and Darrell M. West, Monday November 7, 2016; Accessed on 6 Dec 2021)https://www.brookings.edu/blog/techtank/2016/11/07/the-internet-as-a-human-right/
3. The Process of Protect Humanity; (John Kathil) International Journal of Legal Sphere.

CHAPTER FIVE

THEORY OF SUICIDE GIVEN BY DURKHEIM - PIYUSH PANDEY

Student of Chandigarh University, Mohali.

Suicide is a very complex problem caused by a variety of complex factors. Failure to meet the expectations of a person who may have been implanted at an early age can lead to a variety of suicides that lead to suicide for various reasons. Depression, physical or sexual abuse, depression, financial loss, mental or emotional distress, all of these create feelings of worthlessness and hopelessness and are just a few of the psychological factors that can influence a person's final and distorted decision to commit suicide as a way to end these unbearable feelings. The above, however, is an unfounded analysis that touches on a deeper source of suicide. This paper will attempt to provide a detailed analysis of why people commit suicide by looking primarily at social factors and especially Durkheim's work. Durkheim describes suicide as "a common form of depression and acute pain, which causes the patient to forget the bonds between people and things about him - happiness is no longer attractive". Durkheim went on to say that "a person cannot follow high standards and obey the law if he does not see anything beyond him that can free him from all social pressures to free him and discourage him"

In Durkheim's "Interdiction to Suicide: A Study in Sociology", Durkheim expresses his concern for improving social performance. He sees the great problem that socialism is built primarily on the philosophical point of view, and does not answer direct social questions. proposes a method that will give social science a solid foundation and real results. In his book, Durkheim uses these suggestions and shows how community action should be taken, and he strongly affirmed the conclusions that show us how we should be able to deal with social problems. This study was presented in such a way that it is possible to check the validity and accuracy of their definitions and diagrams. Durkheim emphasizes the importance of social science in addition to being a tool for world development, but it is this, in which we see truth as shared truth, incorporated into people who are committed to their truth. In this introductory chapter, he investigates the act of suicide and examines its origins in society by examining suicide rates at various levels of society and linking them to social indicators.

A distinction is made between two types of suicide, the good and the bad. In Durkheim's words suicide is defined as "all cases of death directly or indirectly from the good or bad deeds of the victim himself, who we know will produce this effect". Good performance can be to remove or stop the action. In this case, death comes as a direct result of the action. A bad act can be a situation of living in a burning house or refusing to eat until you are hungry. Death in this case is a direct result of human actions. Durkheim believes that areas with high levels of mental illness and alcohol abuse are not high-risk areas, esquirol wrote that "suicide may appear to be the only condition for us from many different causes and many different types, and this condition is not a disease". Durkheim believed that suicide was not a personal act or personal achievement. It is produced by supernatural forces.

Durkheim studied suicide due to interpersonal relationships and confirmed that suicide is a social phenomenon and confirmed that there are no societies where suicide does not occur. He emphasized that what many people consider to be the result of social unrest is a result of social unrest. The evidence is overwhelming. In addition to the first difference between good or bad suicide habits, Durkheim's research concludes that the marital institution prevents suicide and raises suicide rates for people who have lost their spouses and for those who have divorced ... that one needs to be loved and to have a purpose in life. People who do not see this in their lives are at risk of suicide. The institution of marriage can thus play an important role in suicidal decisions even if the marriage should be properly considered in relation to suicide but not be corrected. While marriage may play a role in preventing suicide by giving love, purpose and stability to one's life, on the other hand, it can be a fragile institution that has been devastated and could even be the cause of suicide. Durkheim also noted that suicide rates are higher during peacetime than during wartime because, during wartime, people must unite to defend their country. These observations may suggest that feelings of patriotism, respect, and intent often lead to suicide. Suicide rates also tend to be higher during the rapid economic transition than the economic crisis as rapid economic changes are sudden and difficult to bear. Durkheim's comments may suggest that people need to work hard in those economic times and go beyond their limits in order to cope with the rapid changes that are causing such feelings of despair, instability, and ingratitude.

According to Durkheim's research, religion may play a role in suicide rates. The data collected by Durkheim suggested that Protestants were more likely to commit suicide than Catholics because Protestants were stupid while Catholics loved society. In other words, Catholics are inclined to receive public support. According to Durkheim people social cohesion and integration play an important role in suicide prevention which makes this type of social cohesion important. Without this kind of communication, people can experience feelings of depression, loneliness and suicide. Durkheim, however, has been shown pointing to both sides of social cohesion-related socialism that shows that when social cohesion is high, people are more likely to commit suicide to avoid being a burden on society. . Two distinct features are therefore identified by Durkheim; that is, social law and social cohesion. Consolidation is defined as "the level at which the feelings of all people are shared" and the regulation refers to "the level of external social ills". According to both civil society organizations, four types of suicides were proposed by Durkheim.

Durkheim distinguished between four types of suicide, the first of which was self-inflicted. Grandmother suicide is considered to be the result of a lack of social cohesion and is perpetrated by people who are socially excluded and adequately integrated into social groups and communities, relying more on themselves than on a set of goals and commands. They are not affiliated with the public or are bound in public or in a group. These types of people find themselves powerless to find their place in society and experience problems in adapting to other groups and are ignored or ignored. Suicide is therefore regarded as a solution to loneliness or extreme deprivation, which leads Durkheim to point out that this type of suicide is more common among single people, widows, divorced, childless and those without social, social or social status.

The second type of suicide identified by Durkheim is a rare suicide. Anomic suicide is considered by Durkheim as the humiliation and frustration that occurs when a person passes through large clothing and ultimately due to a lack of social rules. This type of suicide is especially noticeable in times when society is rapidly changing and leading to uncertainty. It is a suicide pattern caused by the sudden and unexpected change that Durkheim discovers that occurs more frequently during rapid economic changes than during the economic crisis. Durkheim clearly appeals that suicide is more likely to be a problem that affects a person's health than suffering. Voluntary suicide is the third type of suicide that has been diagnosed and according to Durkheim this type of suicide occurs when people or groups are very close and intimate, and come from extreme social integration. The other side of the scale is social cohesion where one is so well integrated with society that they choose to sacrifice their lives to fulfill a particular obligation. Voluntary suicide, which is a complex concept, can continue to be divided into three types: voluntary, dangerous and suicidal. Voluntary suicide brings social pressures that can be well-intentioned. This can be seen in Japan where there is a high rate of suicide among students due to stress and high expectations of others and constant pressure to excel in school exams.

The accompanying depression is often suicidal; suicide from the victim's point of view becomes the answer to liberation from the oppression of what society expects people to be: Unselfish suicide occurs when a person commits suicide to save another life. An example is when a firefighter saves a person from a burning fire but the fireman dies as a result. This is an act of heroism and self-sacrifice. It can be argued that there may be errors in the categories as this type of suicide is strongly associated with stressful and stressful life and such an act would be a form of positive action. Compulsory suicide is intended to address the type of suicide where respect and dignity play a major role. For example, women in the background should commit suicide at the funeral of their husbands after the death of their husbands who are not allowed to live again. If such a person persists in life he loses the respect of the community; in some cases, the general respect for the funeral is denied, in other cases, a life of expectation should await him beyond the grave. Durkheim points out that unselfish suicide is part of a "cohesive spirit" for example when the spirit asks you to do something you are obliged to do and that we, in turn, see places where society puts a lot of pressure and expectations of people can force a person to commit suicide. The last type of suicide is accidental suicide. Durkheim discussed this genre briefly because he was seen as an abnormal figure in the real world. Excessive suicide occurs in social situations where a person experiences global persecution from "extreme law" his or her desires were brutally suppressed with oppressive discipline.

These four types of suicides are categorized by the degree of integration and control of people in their surrounding community. According to Durkheim people commit suicide because of a very high or very low relationship or law, Suicide is a social reality and is due to the power of society. People often commit suicide each time a social situation changes from a state of stability. The organization maintains a "joint" and "legal" stability. Durkheim's work has been criticized for a number of reasons, for example, his focus on following and behaving, his waiting attitude and human negligence as an actor, his interpretation of suicide rates. Durkheim's view of suicide is thought to be reinforced by controversy rather than fact. However, he has contributed to the development of social science and beyond the complex framework of theory.

Ending suicide is not an individual act a public act. People commit suicide because they do not have the support of the community or do not feel loved by their families when a person lacks support in their life and no one cares when they feel worthless and this will lead to depression which can lead to suicide, suicide rates related to social cohesion and society.

References:

1. Foundations of Modern Social Theory; Lecture 24 Durkheim on Suicide: (https://oyc.yale.edu/sociology/socy-151/lecture-24)
2. What are the types of suicide given by Durkheim? https://courses.lumenlearning.com/atd-bmcc-sociology/chapter/what-are-the-types-of-suicide-given-by-durkheim/
3. Towards A Suicide Free Society: Identify Suicide Prevention As Public Health Policy Ajai R. Singh and Shakuntala A. Singh (https://www.ncbi.nlm.nih.gov/pmc/articles/PMC3400318/)

CHAPTER SIX

Rajasthan Compulsory Registration Of Marriages Amendment Bill 2021: Analysis – Muskan Narwal

Student of Chandigarh University, Mohali.

"Unity is meaningless without the accompaniment of women. Education is fruitless without educated women and agitation is incomplete without the strength of women." — Dr BR Ambedkar

The opposition Bharatiya Janata Party (BJP) charged on September 17 that the Rajasthan Compulsory Registration of Marriages (Amendment) Bill, 2021, which was passed by voice vote in the state Assembly to amend a 2009 Act on mandatory marriage registration within 30 days of the union, will legitimize child marriages.

What Does The Bill State?

On 17 September, the Rajasthan Assembly passed the Rajasthan Compulsory Registration of Marriages (Amendment) Bill, 2021, which changes the Rajasthan Compulsory Registration of Marriages Act, 2009, and requires parents or guardians to provide information on child marriages within 30 days after the wedding.

The Bharatiya Janata Party (BJP) questioned the need for child marriage registration and asked that the law be withdrawn. "How can they include child marriage in this Bill if child marriage is prohibited? All of this is done by Congress in order to create a vote bank." If this measure passes, the assembly will have a bad day. Is it possible for the assembly to agree to legalize child marriages? We shall approve child weddings by a show of hands. The bill would write a dark chapter in the assembly's history. Ashok, a BJP MLA.

The BJP questioned the need for child marriage registration and asked that the law be withdrawn "How can they include child marriage" in the Bill if child marriage is prohibited? All of this is done by congress in order to create a vote bank." If this measure passes the assembly will have bad days. Is it possible for the assembly to agree to legal child marriage? We shall approve child wedding by a show of hands. The bill would write a dark chapter in the assembly's history. Ashok, BJP MLA.

Permitting registration of 'Child marriage' would be detrimental to a civilized society, as it is tantamount to give legality to permits the parties, who have not attained the marriageable age to solemnize the marriage, which is otherwise not permissible and is a punishable offense as envisaged under section 9 ' The Prohibition Of ChildMarriage, 2006'. The object is to punish males who contract marriage with a minor girl.

Questioning the legislative competency to enact such a Bill, the plea submitted that registration of marriage would come within the ambit of the expression "Vital Statics" in Schedule Vll List lll Entry 30 of the constitution of India. Therefore state government does not have legislative competence of vital issues relating to compulsory registration of marriage, it was contended future

According To Section 9 (Prohibition Of Child Marriage 2006)

Whoever, being a male adult above eighteen years of age, contracts a child marriage shall be punishable with rigorous imprisonment which may extend to two years or with a fine which may extend to one lakh rupees or with both.

According To Section 11 (Punishment For Promoting Or Permitting Solemnisation Of Child Marriage)

(1) Where a child contracts a child marriage, any person having charge of the child, whether a parent or guardian or any other person or in any other capacity, lawful or unlawful, including any member of an organization or association of persons who does any act to promote the marriage or permits it to be solemnized, or negligently fails to prevent it from being solemnized, including attending or participating in child marriage, shall be punishable with rigorous imprisonment which may extend to two years and shall also be liable to fine which may extend up to one lakh rupees:

Provided that no woman shall be punishable with imprisonment.

(2) For the purposes of this section, it shall be presumed, unless and until the contrary is proved, that where a minor child has contracted a marriage, the person having charge of such minor child has negligently failed to prevent the marriage from being solemnized.

Child Protection Laws and Benefits of Registration of Child Marriages

The Amendment bill does not contravene child protection legislation like the Prohibition of Child Marriage Act ("Central Act"), Juvenile Justice Act, and Child Marriage Restraint Act. Child marriage is still an offense and registration of such marriages is not tantamount to permitting them. The opponents of this bill argue that it contravenes sections 8, 9, 11, and 12 of the Central Act which provides punishment for promotion and solemnization of child marriages. However, registration of child marriages does not imply that these marriages are legally valid. The marriage registrars can intimate the Child Marriage Prohibition officers when child marriages are registered. Registering child marriages will also assist in prosecuting those individuals who have solemnized or promoted such marriages. The Kerala high court in Punarjani Charitable Trust v. the State Of Kerala held that the state should ensure adequate proof and increased transparency while penalizing offenders under the Central Act. Therefore, the Rajasthan Government should ensure that they have instructed the marriage registrars about alerting the prohibition officers.

Child marriages in India are not void ab initio; they are voidable at the option of the contracting party who was a child at the time of marriage. The petition to annul the marriage has to be filed within two years after attaining majority. While rights and obligations subsist even after divorce, there are no rights and obligations after the annulment of a marriage. However, in order to financially stabilize the female contracting party after the annulment, Section 4 of the Act provides for maintenance and residence to the female contracting party until her remarriage. Registration of child marriages allows the minors to assert their legal rights and prevent the other party from denying the marriage at a later stage. The compulsory registration creates documental evidence of the marriage which facilitates access to benefits available under the Central Act. Therefore, registration of child marriages assists in achieving the objectives sought under the Central Act.

Conclusion

In the end, we can conclude that through this amendment, the transparency of the total number of marriages in the country will be revealed easily. It will be easy to count child marriages and later on lawful action can be taken against those who are encouraging or promoting child marriages.

Reference:

1. Prohibition of child marriages act 2006); Section 9 and section 11 (https://legislative.gov.in/sites/default/files/A2007-06.pdf)
2. Rajasthan Govt To Withdraw the Disputed Marriage Registration Bill (https://www.thequint.com/news/india/rajasthanashok-gehlot-government-disput ed-marriage-registration-bill)

www.ingramcontent.com/pod-product-compliance
Lightning Source LLC
Chambersburg PA
CBHW050622160726
48003CB00003B/1290